★ ★

EXPLORERS OF AMERICA

lewis and clark

WESTERN TRAILBLAZERS

MATTHEW G. GRANT

Illustrated by John Keely and Don Pulver

GALLERY OF GREAT AMERICANS SERIES

★ ★

lewis and clark

WESTERN TRAILBLAZERS

Library of Congress Number: 73-14582   ISBN: 0-87191-277-5

Published by Creative Education, Mankato, Minnesota 56001

LIBRARY OF CONGRESS CATALOGING IN PUBLICATION DATA
Grant, Matthew G
  Lewis and Clark.
  (Explorers in America) (Gallery of great American[s] series)
  SUMMARY: An easy-to-read account of the expedition to explore the Louisiana Territory and the two men who led it.
  1. Lewis and Clark Expedition—Juvenile literature. 2. Lewis, Meriwether, 1774-1809—Juvenile literature. 3. Clark, William, 1770-1838—Juvenile literature. [1. Lewis and Clark Expedition. 2. Lewis, Meriwether, 1774-1809. 3. Clark, William, 1770-1838] I. Keely, John, illus. II. Title.
F592.7.G72 917.8'04'2 [920] 73-14582
ISBN 0-87191-277-5

CONTENTS

THE LEWIS AND CLARK EXPEDITIONS —
1804 — 1806

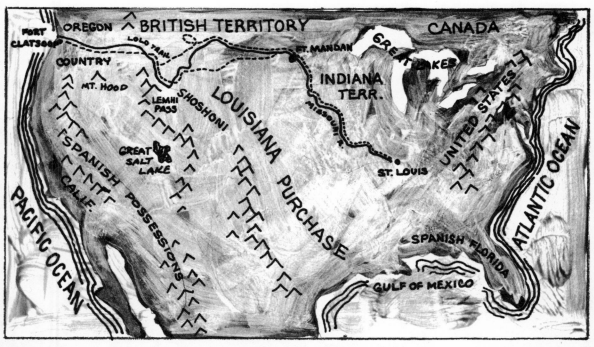

——————— LEWIS AND CLARK, 1804 – 1806

– – – – – LEWIS AND CLARK, RETURN ROUTES

TWO VIRGINIA BOYS

Meriwether Lewis and William Clark were born in Virginia during the early days of the American Revolution. They did not know each other as children. But they grew up to be partners in a great adventure.

William Clark, born in 1770, was a lively red-head. His older brother was the famous General George Rogers Clark, a war hero. In 1783, Congressman Thomas Jefferson talked to General Clark about exploring the unknown West, crossing the Rockies, and reaching the Pacific Ocean.

General Clark would not undertake the trip. He could hardly have dreamed that his

little brother would make the exploration 20 years later.

Meriwether Lewis was born in 1774. His family were neighbors to Thomas Jefferson, who took a great liking to young Meriwether.

At the age of 18, Meriwether Lewis begged Jefferson to send him on an exploration party heading West. But Jefferson thought Lewis was too young. Lewis joined the army

and went off to fight Indians. About 1795, he served in a unit commanded by Captain William Clark.

The two young men became close friends, but they soon separated. Clark returned to his family's farm lands in Kentucky. Lewis followed his army career.

In 1801, Thomas Jefferson became President. He asked Meriwether Lewis to be his private secretary. Jefferson had Lewis start planning a western expedition about 1802. In summer of the next year, Lewis was ready to start. He wrote to his friend Clark, inviting him to come along.

The mails were slow. By the time Clark accepted, the United States had bought the vast Louisiana Territory from France. Lewis and Clark would be the first official party to explore the Louisiana Purchase.

Lewis picked up Clark and his black slave, York, at Louisville. They boated down the Ohio and up the Mississippi to the mouth of the Missouri River. There they spent the winter making final preparations.

UP THE MISSOURI

The "Corps of Discovery" set out on May 14, 1804. They had a keelboat and two large dugouts. Lewis and Clark were co-commanders of a 29-man party. Six soldiers and ten French boatmen would travel partway up the river.

The men rowed and sailed against the current of the wide Missouri. They had to dodge sandbars and floating trees. Sometimes trappers rafted past them with loads of furs. They persuaded one of them, Pierre Dorion, to go North with them and help contact the fierce Sioux.

Near the present site of Sioux City, Iowa, the expedition suffered its first and last death. Sgt. Charles Floyd died of appendicitis.

They passed into buffalo country and met peacefully with a band of Yankton Sioux. But more warlike branches of the tribe awaited them upriver. Toward the end of September they had trouble with the Teton Sioux, who tried to stop them because they were not given enough presents. Lewis and Clark had a cannon on the keelboat and muskets on the dugouts. They faced the Indians to a standoff. Finally a fragile sort of truce prevailed.

JOURNEYS WITH SACAJAWEA

In October they reached the land of the Mandans, in North Dakota. There they built a fort and prepared to spend the winter. Soon they had visitors—a trapper named Toussaint Charbonneau and his Indian wife.

Charbonneau was looking for work and he was hired to interpret. But Lewis and Clark were far more interested in the trapper's Indian wife. Her name was Sacajawea. She was a Shoshoni from the faraway Rocky Mountains. Perhaps she could help the expedition obtain horses from her tribe. Without horses, the expedition could not cross the Rockies.

That winter, Sacajawea gave birth to a baby boy. The next spring she and her child set off with the explorers.

Legends have made Sacajawea a guide. But she was really unable to help Lewis and Clark very much in finding their way. She did help them in another way, however. When Indians watched the expedition pass, they saw a woman and her baby among the men. The Indians then knew that the explorers were not a war party. So they did not attack. The presence of Sacajawea insured that the rest of the journey would be made in peace.

In May, 1805 Lewis and Clark were traveling in Montana. The country was full of elk, deer, and antelope. And there were grizzly bears as well.

A boat accident almost ruined the expedition. A wind came up and tipped the dugout that contained all the papers, books, medicines, and scientific instruments. Fortunately the dugout did not sink. And Sacajawea, who narrowly escaped drowning, helped save the equipment.

In late July they came to the Three Forks of the Missouri. Sacajawea said they were now in the hunting grounds of her people.

Two weeks later, Lewis, in a scouting party, met with the Shoshoni chief, Cameahwait. A few days later, Clark came up with Sacajawea and the rest of the party.

The Indian woman gave a loud cry, then threw her arms around Cameahwait. He was her brother.

Cameahwait warned the explorers that high mountains lay ahead, with little game for the party to eat. Also, winter came early to the high country. The Shoshoni chief traded them 29 horses and a mule and sent five Indian men along to guide them along the Lolo Trail, which led through the heart of the mountains.

They set out on August 30. By September 16 the trail was deep in snow.

THE OREGON COUNTRY

After a terrible journey, they arrived safely in the land of the Nez Perce tribe. The Indians were friendly and told them that the Columbia River was a week's journey to the west.

They made dugouts and sailed down the Clearwater to the Snake River, where they ran high rapids. On October 16, they reached the Columbia. On November 7, 1805, Clark wrote in his diary: "Ocian in view! O! the joy!"

They built a log house, Fort Clatsop, on the Oregon shore. There they spent a hungry, rainy winter. But the Charbonneau baby, Jean-Baptiste, helped to keep up their spirits as they planned the long trip home.

They started back in March, 1806. At the Lolo Trail, the party split up. Clark, most of the men, and Sacajawea took a southerly route. Lewis went to explore the land to the north. They met again on the Missouri River on August 12 and proceeded to Fort Mandan.

Then they said good-bye to Charbonneau, Sacajawea, and the baby. The rest of the Corps of Discovery sailed to St. Louis,

where they were greeted as heroes.

Lewis and Clark traveled some 7,690 miles. Their explorations not only blazed a trail but also enabled the U.S. to claim the Oregon Country in later years.

Lewis became governor of Louisiana Territory. He died in 1809. Clark was governor of Missouri Territory and served as Superintendent of Indian Affairs. He died in 1838. Sacajawea eventually returned to the Shoshoni. Her son, Jean-Baptiste, grew up to be a famous guide.

★ ★
GALLERY OF GREAT AMERICANS SERIES
★ ★

INDIANS OF AMERICA
- GERONIMO
- CRAZY HORSE
- CHIEF JOSEPH
- PONTIAC
- SQUANTO
- OSCEOLA

EXPLORERS OF AMERICA
- COLUMBUS
- LEIF ERICSON
- DeSOTO
- LEWIS AND CLARK
- CHAMPLAIN
- CORONADO

FRONTIERSMEN OF AMERICA
- DANIEL BOONE
- BUFFALO BILL
- JIM BRIDGER
- FRANCIS MARION
- DAVY CROCKETT
- KIT CARSON

WAR HEROES OF AMERICA
- JOHN PAUL JONES
- PAUL REVERE
- ROBERT E. LEE
- ULYSSES S. GRANT
- SAM HOUSTON
- LAFAYETTE

WOMEN OF AMERICA
- CLARA BARTON
- JANE ADDAMS
- ELIZABETH BLACKWELL
- HARRIET TUBMAN
- SUSAN B. ANTHONY
- DOLLEY MADISON

★ ★